YOUR KNOWLEDGE HAS VALUE

D1810106

- We will publish your bachelor's and master's thesis, essays and papers

- Your own eBook and book - sold worldwide in all relevant shops

- Earn money with each sale

Upload your text at www.GRIN.com
and publish for free

Bibliographic information published by the German National Library:

The German National Library lists this publication in the National Bibliography; detailed bibliographic data are available on the Internet at http://dnb.dnb.de .

Imprint:

Copyright © 2015 GRIN Verlag, Open Publishing GmbH
Print and binding: Books on Demand GmbH, Norderstedt Germany
ISBN: 978-3-668-12422-6

This book at GRIN:

http://www.grin.com/en/e-book/313514/evolving-a-new-model-of-health-care-evaluation-in-india

Dipayan Chowdhury

Evolving a new model of Health Care Evaluation in India

GRIN Publishing

GRIN - Your knowledge has value

Since its foundation in 1998, GRIN has specialized in publishing academic texts by students, college teachers and other academics as e-book and printed book. The website www.grin.com is an ideal platform for presenting term papers, final papers, scientific essays, dissertations and specialist books.

Visit us on the internet:

http://www.grin.com/

http://www.facebook.com/grincom

http://www.twitter.com/grin_com

Evolving a new model of
Health Care Evaluation in India

by

Dipayan Chowdhury

Symbiosis Law School, Pune

Symbiosis International University

Acknowledgement

I thank, first and formost, my grandfather, Mr. Kali Prasad Chowdhury, and my adored father, Mr. Usha Kiran Chowdhury, for having endowed me with their respective contributions of the spectacular gift of writing. Everything that I write today and have written owe their origins almost entirely to the inspiration which I have received from these two gentlemen, since I was very small indeed. I thank my beloved mother, Mrs. Paramita Chowdhury, my grandmother, Mrs. Mira Chowdhury, and my dearest sister, Miss Koyel Chowdhury, for having always shown me their continued support, love and encouragement. I give thanks to my dear aunt, Mrs. Krishna Ghosh, for her very important contribution of having inspired me to read as a child. I thank my two special friends, Elke and Sagata, for having been there to hold me when I fell. I also proclaim my sincere gratitude to my professor at University, Mr. Amol Sapatnekar, and to my friend, Mr. Rounak Biswas, for having shared with me their valuable inputs during the course of this study. Lastly, I thank an unnamed individual for having inspired me with a sense of self that I would not have ever either recognized or seen had our paths traversed in different directions. This is an important manuscript, and I therefore acknowledge its readers as well, in the hope that they will read it with interest and will take their respective learnings from the same.

Table of Contents

Abstract

The objective of this study is to analyze the growing implications of malpractice litigation on the evolution of health care reform in India and to further examine the interdependence of the two. The study is specifically in the context of a recent judgment in the Indian Supreme Court, Dr. Balram Prasad v. Doctor Kunal Saha & Ors.[1], where a 770 million rupees compensation had been awarded to the claimant of the suit, on account of certain special circumstances which will be later discussed. The current study attempts to argue, through a combination of medico-legal interpretation and analysis, about the need for adopting equitable justice as the only suitable yardstick for assessing patient care in India in light of the circumstances mentioned. Through the research that has been conducted in this study it has been found that the existing loopholes in the Indian health care model can be requisitely compensated if only the comparative adoption of such policies and principles is allowed in a manner as may be appropriate to the medical health climate in India. This study has already been presented at the International Conference on Comparative Law and Development held in the Indian Society of International Law and organized by the Faculty of Law, Delhi University on the 22nd of March, 2014. Many of the interlinking issues that have been presented in this study are a reflection of the author's own experiences or observations during the years. The author[*] is presently a student of law at the Symbiosis Law School in Pune, India, and has only recently completed an internship under the aegis of the 2014 'L'Ordre national du Mérite' winner, Senior Supreme Court Advocate-on-record & current Additional Solicitor General of India, Mrs. Pinky Anand, as well as a brief period of voluntary service at the Nirmal Hriday Hospice (or Home for the Dying) Branch of the Missionaries of Charity in Kalighat, Kolkata.

---

*Dipayan Chowdhury <d.chowdhury1993@gmail.com>
[1] 2012 (1) CPR 154 (NC)

1

Chapter I. Introduction

Over the last few years, there has been a considerable development in the area of medical malpractice litigation in the Indian subcontinent, a system which has largely been marked by its inordinate delays, exorbitant expenses and little relief for the victims of fraudulent clinical treatment procedures.

The English common law being the original basis for the law on medical negligence in India as felt today, the development has been both inclusive as well as exclusive of parallel deliberations in common law jurisdictions. Furthermore, the emergence of certain notable principles of medical jurisprudence has been observed through the years that are the product of an increasing use of creative interpretation by judges and are not as such specific to only the Indian framework of negligence law.

Only when these principles are read in consonance with the existing legislations regulating the conduct of medical practitioners as well as the recent trends in medical science, can a totality in health care evaluation be achieved. Health care reform in India today stands at an intricate crossroad with the corresponding developments in malpractice litigation whereby policy initiatives and judicial propositions grow interdependently of one another.

The case of *Dr. Balram Prasad v. Doctor Kunal Saha & Ors.*[2] (hereinafter sometimes referred as the *Anuradha Saha* judgment or the case of *Anuradha Saha* or, simply, the judgment) involves an NRI patient, Mrs. Anuradha Saha, who had come to India to visit her mother in Kolkata.

While on her visit, Anuradha began suffering from a skin disease which later gave rise to a few rashes that would appear on her skin. On her first visit to the doctor, she was diagnosed with inflammatory *vasculitis* and was not prescribed any medicine, although it would later turn out that she had actually been suffering from *Toxic Epidermal Necrolysis (TEN)*, which is an extremely rare form of disease.

Over a period of time, the rashes on her skin started rapidly spreading to the other parts of her body and she was thereafter put under a heavy dose of steroid medication. Her condition nevertheless continued to deteriorate following which she was admitted at the AMRI hospital. Subsequent to her treatment at the AMRI hospital , where she could not be cured of her rashes, Anuradha was shifted to a hospital in Mumbai called Breach Candy Hospital; she succumbed to her illness thereafter and died a slow, brutal death.

---

[2] Supra note 1

Chapter II. Revolutionizing the present evidential rule of procedure

One of the most notable observations of the Supreme Court in its judgment on *Anuradha Saha's*[3] case is that, in matters of criminal justice, with respect to the victims of medical negligence, a court will not be bound by the evidence of an expert as such evidence is only advisory in nature and that the court must therefore derive its own conclusion. This observation marks a decisive shift from the *Bolam*[4] standard, which had remained the sole test for determining negligence until now, to the *Bolitho*[5] standard which is a much newer principle in comparison to the former.

While the *Bolam*[6] test dictated that the evidence brought out in support of one's claim of negligent conduct on part of the doctor should have been attestable to a responsible body of medical opinion, the *Bolitho*[7] test requires the evidence to be susceptible to a process of logical interpretation by the judges. However, this shift towards the acceptance of a new standard, for determining negligence still fails to take into account the feasibility of

---

[3] Supra notes 2 and 1
[4] [1957] 1 WLR 583
[5] [1997] 3 WLR 1151
[6] Supra note 4
[7] Supra note 5

production of expert medical evidence in a court of law. This feasibility is in question because of the exorbitant expenses that are usually incurred in the process of gathering such evidence as also the inevitable bias that must arise in the testimonies of physicians who may, for all purposes of our presumption, belong to the same fraternity of doctors as the respondent doctor himself.

Since the initial diagnosis of Anuradha was that of inflammatory *vasculitis*, Dr. Mukherjee, one of the treating doctors at AMRI, was the first to be examined as to how he had sought to treat the same and, subsequently, the High Court accepted his mode of treatment on the basis of evidence adduced by a single expert physician, in complete negligence of the protocols that were otherwise clearly entrenched in the contemporary medical literature on inflammatory *vasculitis* at the time.

Vasculitis is a disease consisting of *protean* clinical manifestations[8] and its origin can only be concluded through an extensive examination of the symptoms. The disease may be *idiopathic*[9] i.e., a disease whose cause of growth is unknown, or may be associated with a spectrum of condition such as drugs, infections, etc. Also, the existing treatment line for *vasculitis* is highly disputed and is

---

[8]Pooja Khetan, Gomathy Sethuraman, Binod K. Khaitan, Vinod K. Sharma, Rajeeva Gupta Amit K. Dinda,V. Sreenivas and Manoj K. Singh, An aetiological & clinicopathological study on cutaneous vasculitis, Indian Journal of Medical Research, Volume 135, Pages 107-113 (January, 2012)
[9] Ibid.

thereby expected to be established in different ways and variations through further clinical research into the area. The testament in favour of Dr. Mukherjee's chosen method of treating inflammatory *vasculitis* stands verily unqualified therefore in respect of the blatant exclusion of any academic reference.

Furthermore, according to Vasculitis UK, a respectable charity trust founded in the year 1992 and since conducting independent research on the said disease, the treatment for *vasculitis* has to be conducted in two phases, namely, remission induction therapy and remission maintenance therapy, either of which has to be supported by the other, where steroid administration has to be followed by additional treatment of *cyclophosphamide*[10] in order to control the infections resulting from the *immunosuppressive* action of the drugs, and where the initial steroid dosage has also to be gradually reduced to a bare minimum at a certain point.

While the administration of *prednisolone* was corroborated by the physician expert, the failure to provide a supportive treatment by way of *cyclophosphamide* application was never touched upon by the court or the attending experts owing to which the very criminal omission on part of the respondent Dr. Mukherjee was blithely overlooked. What

---

[10] Vandana D Pradhan and Kanjaksha Ghosh, Anti-Idiotype Antibodies in Immune Regulation of ANCA Association of Vasculitis, Indian Journal of Dermatology, Volume 54, Issue 3, Pages 258-262, (July-September, 2009)

impact this may have on prospective negligence suits arising out of the maltreatment of *vasculitis*, a disease which bears a distinctly minimal survival rate, is yet to be realized in the coming future.

There are other cases, paralleling similar situations or conditions to the present case, which if read leads us to question and thereby implore as to what extent the evidence produced by experts can be considered accountable. One of such cases include *R.K. Agarwal v. Dr. B. Mukhupadhay*[11] where the plaintiff after accidentally fracturing his hand consulted a physician whose suggested treatment the plaintiff eventually withdrew from at a later stage. He thereafter consulted another physician who gave a different opinion that was not on record and the plaintiff subsequently became disabled, even after having meticulously followed through with the advice that had been renderedto him. The court could not decide as to which form of treatment would have been correct and the case was dismissed thereof.

In *Farangilal Mutneja vs. Shri Guru Harkishan Sahib Eye Hospital Sahana and Anr.*[12], the Union Territory Commission, Chandigarh dismissed the claim based on medical negligence by observing that subsequent to the eye operation that was performed on the plaintiff by the

---

[11]I (1995) CPJ 260
[12]IV (2006) CPJ 96

operating physician (O.P.) the cornea had become damaged and the person's visibility was lost as a result.

The complainant alleged that proper dilation of the eyes had not been ascertained before conducting the cataract operation. It was also alleged that the operation was conducted in an extremely hastened manner. The Medical Council of India, after obtaining the expert opinion of two well-known institutions, came to the conclusion that standard treatment protocol was followed and optimal procedures were carried out. Thus, the O.P. was not held liable for the charge of negligence and the suit was thereof dismissed.

Bearing the above cases in mind, a suitable alternative to the use of expert physician testimony is seen to be much wanting in the field of medical jurisprudence. One such an alternative could be to enforce the admission of relevant medical literature, examples being Computerized Tomography (CT) scan reports, post mortem reports, Central Forensic Science Laboratory (CFSL) reports, text books on medical health issues and the like, all of which may be accorded the same status as that of expert medical testimony, classified[13] by the word "opinion" under Section 45 of the Indian Evidence Act.

The court has said that the law on medical negligence needs to be in tune with the modern developments in medical

---

[13] Jaising P. Modi, A Text Book of Medical Jurisprudence and Toxicology, Lexis NexisButterworths, 24th edn. (2011)

science, treatment as also diagnostics. Keeping in line with this observation, it may be said that modern academic research indeed seems to be the right choice in terms of determining ethical medical treatment standards, as against a system of admitting evidence where it is difficult even to ascertain whether the expert examining the qualification of evidence has at least a sufficient knowledge in the more recently advancing areas of medical science.

In *P. Venkata Lakshmi vs. Dr. Y. Savita Devi*[14], where the plaintiff had filed a negligence suit for the refusal of induction despite persistent labour pains as also neo-natal complications suffered prior to the delivery, the National Commission held that the State Commission ought to have paid a reasonable consideration to the medical literature as had been initially filed by the complainant and which had been previously dismissed on the grounds of failure to produce expert evidence.

In *Consumer Protection Council & Ors. v Dr. M. Sundaram &Anr.*[15], the facts of which consists of a peculiar similarity to the manner in which Anuradha was misdiagnosed and subsequently maltreated, a medicinal compound known as *Endoxan* had been used to treat a patient suffering from *Hodgkin's Lymphoma*. This was done although, according to the relevant medical literature at the time, *Endoxan* was to be used strictly for the purpose of treating *non-Hodgkin's*

---

[14] II (2004) CPJ 14 (NC)
[15] 1998 2 CPJ 3 (NC)

Lymphoma and not *Hodgkin's Lymphoma*, there being a critical difference between the two classes of disease in that *Hodgkin's Lymphoma* would be characterized by the presence of a very specific type of abnormal cell, called a *Reed-Sternberg cell*, which would be otherwise absent in a person suffering from *non-Hodgkin's lymphoma*.

Now, having discussed the above cases, explicating around the same set of facts or the similar nature of circumstances, it becomes necessary to implore the possible courses of corrective actions. There are two measures which may specifically be discussed in the particular context of the situations mentioned; they are, firstly, making the production of expert opinion a non-mandatory process[16] and, secondly, instituting academicians, considering their frequent engagement in dialogue with the medical community, as well as people belonging to the non-medical backgrounds, or basically 'lay people' in plain usage, selected from a wide range of social activities[17], as members of the Indian Medical Council (IMC)[18]. The only distinguishing factor would be here that this latter class of persons, as has just been mentioned above, will have at some point been witnesses to the realities of the Indian

---

[16] Gregory Durston, Evidence: Text & Materials, Oxford University Press, Pages 462-463 (2013)
[17] Seventy-third Report on The Indian Medical Council (Amendment) Bill 2013, Ministry of Health and Family Welfare, as presented to the Rajya Sabha on 20th November, 2013
[18] Sixtieth Report on The National Commission for Human Resources for Health Bill 2011, Department Related Parliamentary Standing Committee on Health and Family Welfare, as presented to the Hon'ble Chairman of the Rajya Sabha on 30th October 2012

health care system in a much more practical and real sense than usual.

Moving onto the year of 1993, in the landmark case of *Daubert v. Merrell Dow Pharmaceuticals, Inc.*[19], a single U.S. Supreme Court Judge had remarkably established, setting new rules in favour of evidence procurement, that for scientific evidence to be admissible in court, it must first be amenable to testing, should undergo peer review publication, should have known potential error rates, and should be generally accepted in the scientific community. The *Daubert* precedent now applies to expert testimony in all federal courts, and under this standard, the presiding bench must evaluate expert testimony, whether medical or otherwise, to ensure that it is both relevant and reliable.

In another landmark case originating in England, namely, *McAllister v Lewisham & N Southwark HA*[20], it was held by the House of Lords that a judge may render medical 'opinion' a broad interpretation, in order to incorporate the totality of medical evidence available to the court, including the results of diagnostic tests and observations in authoritative medical works.

Although Kunal had arranged for the deposition of three international authors, conducting independent research on *TEN*, via a video communication service device, since the authors were settled abroad at the time, the Supreme Court,

---

[19] 509 U.S. 579 (1993)
[20] [1994] 5 Med LR

rendering a restrictive version of the appealed High Court verdict, observed that a video conference can indeed be presented as a mode of evidence during the proceedings of a civil court but that the same cannot be maintainable during the proceedings of a criminal court.

However, the same court, in *State v. S.J. Chowdhary*[21], had taken an entirely different approach towards the interpretive cognizance of medical evidence when Justice J.S. Verma had made the observation that for every interpretation of an Act there is a presumption of updated construction and, hence, every new technique or scientific advancement in any field is well within the scope of expert evidence in Section 45 of the Indian Evidence Act and that the words 'science' or 'art' within the meaning of the said Section under the Act has to be very widely construed.

It is an admitabble position therefore to say that in the present case the Indian Supreme Court has failed to live up to the spirit of harmonious construction as arising from its preceding observations, and an infallible opportunity, to address the issue of criminal justice in contemporaneous terms of medical reference, has become salvaged through the Court's unceremonious usage of preferential constructivism and by the deliberate diminution of its jurisdiction.

---

[21] 1996 AIR 1941

Chapter III. De-limiting the patient's right to bodily autonomy

The High Court and the National Commission had absolved liability on part of the doctors for medical negligence on the ground of cleavage in opinion i.e., the evidences produced by the opposite behalves in the suit were equally strong in their individual components, one being in favour of pro-steroid treatment and the other being in favour of anti-steroid treatment. The Supreme Court eventually reversed this decision as held by the above courts by reasoning that even if pro-steroid treatment were to be held as the standard for measuring reasonable care and precaution on part of the defendant doctor the latter had still failed in his duty to maintain the same.

Direct evidence, if found satisfactory and reliable, cannot be rejected on the basis of a mere hypothetical medical assumption.[22] If there is conflict in the opinion of two expert medical witnesses, then the opinion of that medical witness that supports the direct evidence should ordinarily be accepted.[23] Furthermore, the incohesion of two meeting ends in a medical testimony is a problem that has plagued the courts, time and again, in deciding cases revolving

---

[22] Yaqoob Shah v. The State PLD 1976 SC 53; Prem Sagar Manocha v. State (NCT of Delhi), Criminal Appeal No. 9 of 2016
[23] Dr. Parikh and Dr. Mishra, The Principles of Medical Jurisprudence, Medical and Forensic Science and Technology, CBS Publisher & Distributor (2012)

around a myriad range of medical complications, but the essential point of aversion that has surmised in *Anuradha Saha*[24] is of how a crucial doctrine may be rendered inapplicable sometimes by virtue of its simple non-applicability, the non-applicability concerned here being that of a doctrine, which the courts have themselves evolved in past decisions, to a situation where such a doctrine could have been easily and most effectively employed in order to settle the balance between two significantly conflicting probabilities.

While dealing with the aspect of informed consent and a patient's right to be made aware of the risks relating to a particular treatment, the Supreme Court dwelled on the future possibility of litigation being based on a new test for determining liability, which is the theory of lack of informed consent, wherein a stringent standard of disclosure in conjunction with the concept of proximate cause is to be applied.

The concept of proximate cause first originated in the case of *Palsgraf v. Long Island R. Co*[25] where there was a passenger who while attempting to board a running train appeared to be falling to the defendants. The defendants were two station guards, one being positioned on the platform and the other being positioned inside the train itself. The guard who was standing inside the train tried to pull the passenger

---

[24] Supra notes 3, 2 and 1
[25] 248 N.Y. 339

inside while the other guard who was standing on the platform tried to push the passenger into the train from behind. In their attempts to help the passenger, the package that the passenger was carrying, containing fireworks not known to the unsuspecting defendant guards, fell onto the rails leading to a massive explosion thereof. The explosion knocked the scales that were placed on the other side of the platform and the plaintiff, Mrs. Helen Palsgraf, became injured as a result.

Palsgraf sued the railroad, claiming that her injury had resulted from the negligent acts of the employee. The trial court and the intermediate appeals court, by a common opinion from the jury, passed a verdict in favour of the plaintiff, but the defendants appealed the verdict. The Court of Appeals, which is the highest court in New York, reversed and dismissed Palsgraf's complaint, holding that the relationship of the guard's action to Palsgraf's injury was too indirect to make him liable.

However, the three-judge dissent, written by Judge Andrews and joined by Judges Frederick Crane and John F. O'Brien, by contrast, saw the case as a matter of proximate cause where the plaintiff's injury could be immediately traced to the wrong committed by the guard, and it was held that the fact of the wrong and the fact of the injury should be enough to find negligence.

The relevant lesson that we learn from *Palsgraf*[26] and which could have been creatively applied in case of *Anuradha Saha*[27] is that for the defendant to be liable, the wrongfulness of the defendant's risk creation must be correlative to the wrongfulness of the plaintiff's injury; this principle was ultimately not adapted in the judgment.

Meanwhile, the Court, while explaining its position on the doctrine of informed consent, adapted the precedent of *Sidaway v. Bethlem Royal Hospital Governers*[28] instead, which is a landmark judgment but which is otherwise known for its discrepant lack of judicial consensus. In this case, the plaintiff had suffered from an injury to her spinal cord during an operation she was undergoing to free a trapped nerve; she was left partially paralyzed thereafter. Later, an action was instituted by the plaintiff against the treating doctor alleging that the risks involved in her treatment had not been properly explained to her. She said that she had given her consent owing to the negligence of the doctor.

The evidence showed that two specific risks of injury could have occurred to a patient undergoing the operation that was performed on the plaintiff, the first being a damage to the nerve and the second being a damage to the spinal cord. The judge found in light of the facts that the surgeon, Mr. Falconer, had warned the plaintiff of the risk of danger

---

[26] Supra note 22
[27] Supra notes 21
[28] [1985] AC 871

to the nerve but he had said nothing about the possibility of paralysis. The expert witnesses also testified that at the time of the operation some neurosurgeons would have considered it best to keep quiet about the risk of paralysis.

The House of Lords rejected the claim of the plaintiff eventually and the neurosurgeon was not tried for the way in which he had performed the operation since it was believed to be a genuine accident, not a negligent mistake. However, the dissenting opinion of Justice Scarman in the case is absolutely critical. Scarman argued that the patient has a right to take a decision on any action that is affected on her body. He believed that this right to one's bodily autonomy is further supported by a right to be given all the information that is material in deciding whether to accept the treatment that he or she has been advised to have.

If a material risk is not disclosed, then the doctor responsible for treating the patient would be held guilty of negligence. In order to decide whether something is a material consideration, the court should ask whether a reasonable person in the patient's position would have regarded the information as being significant or not. Scarman described this as a 'prudent patient' test. To operate the test in clinical practice, doctors would have to ask themselves what a reasonable and conscionable person in a patient's position would want to know.

Scarman's reasoning reflects in a few other cases originating from common law countries that are of a similar nature and which become important precedents for subsequent cases, such as the case of *Snell v. Farrell*[29] in Canada and the case of *Rhine v. Millan*[30] in the US. In each of these cases, the respective bench had conclusively decided that the interest of the patient would have to be placed on a much higher pedestal in relation to the doctor's duty towards the patient, the duty being to reveal all such information as would be material for the patient to know about the direct and indirect consequences of the treatment.

In *Rhine v. Millan*[31], the plaintiff was diagnosed with *Crohn* disease. She had a very severe form of *Crohn* because of which she had underwent a surgical bowel resection and following this surgery she was put on *intravenous* corticosteroids by her gastroenterologist. The patient was then subsequently switched to another gastroenterologist but she continued to suffer the symptoms of active inflammatory disease and was thus prescribed several oral and *intravenous corticosteroids*. Later, she developed *avascular necrosis (AVN)* in both of her lips and shoulders and, after a passage of time, both of her lips had to be replaced.

---

[29] [1990] 2 SCR 311
[30] [2000] A.J. No. 367
[31] Supra note 27

The patient further began to experience a variety of neurological symptoms and was eventually diagnosed with *multiple sclerosis.* After three years, the plaintiff sued the gastroenterologist claiming that she was not made aware of the potential side effects of the steroids including the *AVN* which she had suffered from and the court eventually ruled in favour of the plaintiff's claim.

On the issue of informed consent, the court applied a test similar to the 'prudent patient' test. The Bench concluded that a reasonable person with the patient's condition would not have consented to the continued treatment with *corticosteroids* had she been made aware of the risk of *avascular necrosis*, although it is a disease with a rare occurence. Liability was finally restored on the respondent gastroenterologist for having made use of an excessive amount of steroid medication while setting aside the aspect of the *AVN* risk although high steroid use is indeed often associated with the cause of *AVN.*

In *Snell v. Farrell*[32], the defendant, Dr. Farrell, had negligently performed eye surgery on the plaintiff, a diabetic with a number of pre-existing health complications. During the course of the surgery, the plaintiff incurred blindness in one of her eyes. She simultaneously experienced a stroke in that same eye, which could also have caused her blindness. Evidence at trial

---

[32] Supra note 26

could not conclusively point to whether or not her blindness was caused by Dr. Farrell's negligence or by the plaintiff's deteriorating health condition.

The Supreme Court of Canada inferred causation on the part of Dr. Farrell. Although the plaintiff could prove that the defendant's negligence may have been a contributing risk factor in the type of injury she had suffered, she could not link that negligence to the actual cause of the injury. Both Dr. Farrell's negligence and the plaintiff's poor health were independent and equally plausible causes of the eventual blindness that the patient would suffer.

Thus, from the description of the above cases, what can be seen is that the material contribution test is adequately applied where the traditional 'but for' test is found unworkable and also, in the medical negligence context, it is applied in specifically those circumstances where the plaintiff's injury is caused by the cumulative effect of two or more factors, at least one of which may be tortious.[33]

Personal autonomy and right to self-determination is increasingly being recognized as a universal human right. The right to self-determination is the fundamental principle of international law. Many recent international human rights documents include rights of self-determination in their lists of basic human rights. This right provides for

---

[33] C.E. Hinkson, Q.C. and M.G. Thomas of Harper Grey LLP, Causation in medical malpractice cases, A paper written by for the Trial Lawyers Association of British Columbia, 2007

individual autonomy, human dignity, self-consciousness and the right to choose.[34]

Personal autonomy being the bulwark, what remains to be seen in the future roadmap of malpractice litigation in India is whether the Courts, keeping with the observation founded in *Anuradha Saha*[35] that 'the human rights of medical negligence victims must be strictly protected', will at all be willing to take a more definitive stand on the *Sidaway*[36] precedent and whether it would even possibly consider accepting the position, as had been espoused by Justice Scarman, towards the granting of an enhanced right of autonomy to the general public in respect of their health.

---

[34] Govind v. State of MP AIR 1975 SC 1378
[35] Supra notes 24 and 21
[36] Supra note 25

Chapter IV. Re-designing medicinal practice to equitable innovation

While deciding on a question relating to the mode of treatment as performed by the respondent doctors, the Supreme Court of India has said that where the physician has to his disposal any number of methods for a particular cause of treatment then the preference of one over the other would not be enough to hold the physician liable for medical malpractice if he has acted with due care and precaution towards the method that he has chosen. However, it has to be remembered here that a patient's right to self-determination and autonomy is not absolute in India and a doctor has no primary obligation to reveal all and any information that an individual patient may demand in order to determine his own acceptance or rejection of the treatment thereof.

Two possibilities for rectification arise here, one being that the selection of treatments be made more streamlined with help of a uniform and standardized medical protocol system or, as per the *Sidaway*[37] proposal, the decision of the doctor is made binding only on the absolute discretion of the patient upon whom the operation is purported to be performed, given that all the possible areas of treatment

---

[37] Supra notes 31 and 25

and the related symptoms which may be reasonably foreseen as arising from the same have been already disclosed to him beforehand.

Nonetheless, as per the common practice which is followed in accordance with the general norms, leaving the doctors with an entirely independent mandate as to how the treatment should be performed often exposes the patient to an unguarded process of exploitation and experimentation whereby the risk of more infections or even a complete failure of treatment is further exacerbated.

The reason is that there is a plentitude of physicians, nowadays, who, under the pretext of acting with due care and precaution, are increasingly resorting to the use of some surreptitious practices, more specifically, practices like defensive medicine or illegal drug trials, which shall be seen to have played their respective roles in the death of Anuradha Saha and shall be discussed in the same vein. The judges ought to have considered the possible existence of such scenarios while formulating their self-centric concept of informed consent, and the significance of why they should have done so will be explored below, although the particular practices mentioned are not penal offences per say.

Now, coming first to the practice of defensive medicine as was mentioned above, defensive medicine can be defined as any act or omission, approved by medical science, on the part of a doctor who is primarily motivated to avoid incurring a liability for medical negligence. It can be categorized into two types, one being negative defensive medicine or negative defensive practice and the other being positive defensive medicine or positive defensive practice; the concepts are also interchangeably referred to, sometimes, as avoidance behaviour and assurance behavior respectively[38].

Negative defensive practice, or avoidance behaviour, in simple parlance, can be described as an act of omission. For example, doctors avoiding giving injection, avoiding risky procedures or operation, avoiding admitting serious patients, etc. Positive defensive practice, or assurance behaviour, on the other hand, is an act ordering additional investigations or procedures which might be avoidable. For example, a physician may advice C.T. scan for every headache or a surgeon may go for all investigations including E.C.G. before performing even a minor operation. It makes the medical treatment more costly as the doctor may insist for hospitalization or for a second opinion. He may do over treatment by doing frequent visits, longer treatments and doing caesarian to avoid risks of prolonged labour.

In Anuradha's case, the repeated performance of tests and diagnostic procedures, the multiple referrals from one

[38]Gayatri Vidya Parishad, Dialogue and Democracy: Reflections on Ideas, Issues and Policy, Centre for Policy Studies, Vishakapatnam, 2nd edtn. (June 2012)

doctor to the other, in addition to the lack of requisite follow ups with each successive treatment, fits in perfectly well with the above named kinds of defections, but they still could not be attributed the nature of any offence belonging to the realm of medical torts.

Now, although a plain perusal of certain sections under the Code of Medical Ethics Regulations Act, 2002, namely, sections 2.3, 2.4 and 3.1, reveals the availability of only a few protective legal provisions against the gargantuan phenomena of defensive medicine, the law in place in India is still insufficient to combat the social menace that is resulting from the practice of the same because defensive medicine, despite its growing relevance over the years, still remains an isolated concept from the accepted definition of medical negligence today and is thus conveniently omitted from the general medico-legal discourse, both within the court as well as the hospital.

The practice of defensive medicine can be tackled, nevertheless, from a legislative point of view, if the doctors, in collaboration with the policy framers, formulate the duly tested procedures of treatment into an ascertainable protocol whereby the need for multiple opinions is completely eliminated.

Here, it appears to be vital to mention the need for adoption of an emerging concept in the field of medicinal science, known as 'evidence based guidelines', given that it is, first, effectively introduced within the Indian medical discourse at the preliminary level and, second, that it receives a positive affirmation from within the medical community.

Among the several existing sources of definition on the concept of evidence based guidelines, we may take cue from the definition that has been recently proposed by the Center for American Progress (C.A.P) to the American Government, the C.A.P being a renowned public policy research and advocacy organization based in the United States. To reduce the costs of defensive medicine, the C.A.P proposes the creation of a "safe harbor"[39] in medical-malpractice litigation that will protect physicians provided that they have documented adherence to a certain specified set of evidence based guidelines, used qualified health information technology systems and worked under the full direction of clinical decision taking support mechanisms.

The legal standard of care, as has been traditionally determined in the U.S., complies with the local customary practices of a physician in a particular community. Such a duty of care is not tenable as treatments may be varying from one community to another and is often found to be unsupported by evidence. Under a safe harbor, guidelines would be presumed to define the legal standard of care.

---

[39] Ezekiel J. Emanuel, Topher Spiro, and Maura Calsyn, Reducing the Cost of Defensive Medicine, Center for American Progress, June 11, 2013

Patients would be able to present evidence that the guidelines were not applicable to the given situation or that a physician did not actually follow the guidelines; they could also use the guidelines to establish negligence by physicians.

The Harvard School of Public Health, in collaboration with an organization known as Common Good and with support provided by the Robert Wood Johnson Foundation of the Commonwealth Fund, released an outline[40] between the years of 2005 and 2006 that again reintroduced the concept of evidence based guidelines. Their idea was that these guidelines would be used to assist the judges in dealing with cases involving composite clinic-legal interactions and especially ones which are particularly unique in their nature of occurrence.

Furthermore, the Institute of Medicine, in a report[41] brought out by it in the year 2001,recommended the creation of an Electronic Health Record System, similar to the one as was aimed to be introduced by the 2004 U.S. Government under the then President George W. Bush. Such a system, bearing parallel resemblance to the way in which an evidence based system operates, would not only

---

[40] Medical Liability: News Idea for Making the System Work Better for Patients, Hearing of the Committee on Health, Education, Labour and Pensions, One Hundredth Ninth Congress, Second Session on Examining Alternatives to Improve the Medical Liability System to work Better for Patients, U.S. Government Printing Office, 22nd June 2006
[41] Crossing the Quality Chasm: A New Health System for the 21st Century, Institute of Medicine, 2001

allow records to be created and stored electronically but would also make these records transmissible through an electronic network serving as the foundation for a comprehensive health IT system.[42]

The other capabilities of the invention being clinical documentation, health information, results management, order-entry management, clinical decision support, electronic communication and connectivity, patient support, administrative processes, reporting and disease surveillance[43], the invention could very well be cited as being a key inspiration for a similar model in India.

Lastly, if we draw upon even the existing domestic authorities in order to support the basis for the creation of an evidence based model of healthcare in India, a very recently adjudged case comes to the fore, *Mrs. Shantaben Muljhibai Patel and Ors. vs. Breach Candy Hospital and Research Centre and Ors.*[44], where the National Commission had referred the judgment delivered by Lord Denning in *Roe and Woolley vs. The Ministry of Health and an Anaesthesist*[45] with approbation. The said judgment provides that every surgical operation is attended by risks, that we cannot take the benefits without taking the risks, that every advance in technique is also attended by risks, and that doctors, like

---

[42] Joel B. Korin and Madelyn S. Quattrone, Litigation in the Decade of Electronic Health Records, New Jersey Law Journal, 2007
[43] Ibid.
[44] I (2005) CPJ 10 (NC)
[45] (1954) 2 All ER 131

the rest of us, have to ultimately learn by experience. The conclusion from this therefore is apparent that evidence indeed arises from experience, and if only there can be a provision whereby individual doctors are able to network their experience and learn from each other's, can potential risks and mistakes be avoided.

Now, moving on to a discussion on the conjoining issue of illegal drug trials, a drug trial is a process involving human subjects where the dosage requirement for a particular drug intervention is studied through an extensive examination of the drug component in the blood of the patient undergoing the study; the examination is usually carried out in three successive phases, namely, phase I, phase II and phase III.[46]

Keeping in consideration that, sometimes, a single term or terminology can be interchangeably used to describe separate concepts and that different terms can similarly be used to discuss the same concept, it must be noted that clinical trials have been discussed here in the nature of innovative treatments[47], these treatments being an inherent feature of medical care, whereby the doctors, at times, modify their operations in light of what they have learnt from their previous experiences of patients and then use it

---

[46]P.R.O. Payne, P.J. Embi, S.B. Johnson, E. Mendonca, and J. Starren, Improving Clinical Trial Participant Tracking Tools Using Knowledge-Anchored Design Methodologies, Applied Clinical Informatics, Volume 1, Issue 2, Pages 177-196 (2010)
[47] Shaun D. Pattinson, Medical Law and Ethics, Sweet and Maxwell, 1stedn. (2006)

to further experiment with the results of, until then, new and untested therapies.

Thus, the principle premise for instituting protection against the performance of illegal clinical trials is that the thin line of difference between medical research, whose main aim is to produce new knowledge for the benefit of future patients, and medical treatment, the aim of which is to benefit the immediate patient, has now disintegrated to such a position as where where the doctor's purportedly overarching intention[48] to treat the patient concerned has become significantly indistinguishable.

One of the contributing factors to the above decribed phenomena could be that many physicians, nowadays, are joining their hands with some of the major players of the pharmaceutical industry, their purpose being to test the drugs that some of these enterprises discreetly manufacture while clearly violating the current market regulations concerning the same.[49]

Even if the regulations controlling the operations of clinical trials are considered in segregation, it is found that they are plainly inadequate when it comes to the question of their implementability. For example, the Clinical Establishment Registration and Regulation Act, as enacted by the Central Government in 2010, does not include in its ambit

---

[48] Ibid.
[49] Batham, Vikash, Rijit Sengupta and Vasanthi Srinivasan, Rethinking Business Responsibility in India: A Review of Pharmaceutical & Private Healthcare Sectors, CUTS International, Jaipur, 2013

independent Research & Development (R & D) operations being conducted in healthcare establishments, including hospitals and private nursing homes, as such establishments are excluded from the definition of 'clinical establishments' under Section 2 (c) of the Act.

Exclusion of R & D operations adds to the detriment of patient care in the country as, unbeknownst to the vulnerable victims of illegal trials, dangerous combinations of drugs are often tried on them in varying intervals and prohibitive quantities. The sitting bench having itself recognized that *Toxic Epidermal Necrolysis*, which the victim was alleged to have been suffering from, is a rare occurring disease with very little reference in existing medical literature, it provides a sufficient reason as to why a proper investigation ought to have been conducted behind the respondent's ill will to continue with the treatment of Anuradha, despite having no adequate proportion knowledge in respect of the disease concerned or even regarding the use of *Depomedrol* for its treatment, clinical data pertaining to the disease being largely non-existant at the time.

Furthermore, the judges in *Anuradha Saha*[50] had also made the recognition that the *imunosuppressive* action resulting from the use of a long-acting steroid would only musk the signs of infection and further give rise to the formation of

---

[50] Supra notes 30 and 24

opportunistic infections instead of showing any real indication of improvement. This could mean that certain treatments may only be having the appearance of a therapeutic intervention when, in actuality, the real therapeutic requirement will have been entirely ignored[51].

However, courts are not equipped with the appropriate terminologies to technically define the grounds of liability which would otherwise emerge from the above aspects, and the judgment, thereby, will inevitably end up working in favour of maltreating doctors in the future on the condition that they are able to demonstrate only an achievable level of diligence in how they operate. Therefore, against the backdrop of a fading clinical research mechanism in India that is already dented with an incessant number of loopholes, what surfaces here is the need for an immediate switch from the current Phase 1 standard method of drug testing that involves human subjects to a more rational alternative that does away with the risks which an average patient could be subject to otherwise and that, moreover, does not require to be enmeshed in the same complex legal protections, the needful being that potential damage involved is significantly less or even negligible.

---

[51]Robert Tenery, Herbert Rakatansky, Frank A. Riddick, Jr., Michael S. Goldrich, Leonard J. Morse, John M. O'Bannon, III, Priscilla Ray, Sherie Smalley, Matthew Weiss, Audiey Kao, Karine Morin, Andrew Maixner and Sam Seiden, Surgical "Placebo" Controls, Annals of Surgery, Volume 235 Issue 2, Pages 303-307 (February, 2002)

Microdosing[52], also known as the *Phase 0* standard, is one such solution that is recently coming up in a few countries, while gaining an increasing international popularity, its purpose being to limit human exposure to the effects of clinical trial. The concept of microdosing involves[53] the use of extremely low, *nonpharmacologically* active doses of a drug to define the *pharmacokinetic* profile of the medication in human subjects; it is not intended to identify or study the maximum tolerable dose in its subject unlike the Phase 1 method of conducting clinical drug trial.

Guidelines issued by the European Medicine Agency (EMEA) and the United States Federal Drug Agency (USFDA) in 2004 and 2006, respectively, have provided recognition to the concept and legitimacy surrounding the conduct of microdosing. However, the Indian law on medical negligence needs to move ahead with the changing conditions in order to be able to accommodate such progressive developments within the field of medical science; this is again a pronouncement that was reiterated in the judgment itself.

Courts would need to read treatments by way of mircodosing, if it is indeed introduced in the country at some point in the near future, as existing outside the

---

[52] Dr. Tushar Tiwari and Dr. Shoibal Mukherjee, Microdosing: Concept, Application and Relevance, Perspectives in Clinical Research., Voume 1, Issue 2, Pages 61-63(April-June, 2010)
[53] P. Usha Rani and M.U.R. Naidu, Phase 0- Microdosing strategy in clinical trial, Indian J. Pharmacol, Vol. 40(6), Nov- Dec 2008

purview of the currently pending Drugs and Cosmetics (Amendment) Bill, 2013. This approach is needed so that the doctors are able to incorporate it within their routine medical practice, being free from the apprehension of liability that elsewise ensues from illegally resorting to unconventional clinical trial procedures.

Under the said Drugs and Cosmetics (Amendment) Bill, 2013, sub-clause (af) under clause (iii) of Section 6 has defined the meaning of clinical trial as a "systematic study of new drug, investigational new drug or bioavailability or bioequivalence study of any drug in human subjects to generate data for discovering or verifying its clinical, pharmacological (including pharmacodynamic and pharmacokinetic) or adverse effects with the objective of determining safety, efficacy or tolerance of the drug". The legal context of this definition with regard to the inclusivity of microdosing is not explicitly encumbered with any form of judicial hindrance. However, a requisite for further expository intervention into the matter by the courts still remains.

Chapter V. Recognizing the need for compliance free package regulations

One of the most critical points in the *Anuradha Saha*[54] judgment is the decision that was held on the question of enforceability in product related guidelines. The court has declared that the "package insert" of a drug i.e., instructions provided for use on the body of the medicine container, must be stringently followed by the doctors and that directions given anywhere else, even in the textbooks, cannot supersede instructions written on the "package insert" of the concerned product. Although, this declaration by the court serves as a strong precedent against the use of excessive drug dosage, it could, however, impose an unduly restriction, in some exceptional situations, on the administration of certain quantities of the drug as may be required by the patient.

In the wake of an increasing move towards the alignment of domestic drug regulation standards with those of international drug monitoring bodies like the USFDA and the EMEA, there appears to be a growing shift in the radicalization of the Indian health care structure. The Drugs and Cosmetics (Amendment) Bill, 2013 lays the foundation of a new Central Drug Authority with a modus

---

[54] Supra notes 45 and 31

operandi on the same lines as that of the FDA[55]. Furthermore, current considerations[56] are also being made to subject the Ethics Committees, as constituted under Section 4(T) under Chapter (IB) of the Bill, to audit inspection by, again, the USFDA and the EMEA. Thus, there was a peremptory requirement in *Anuradha Shah*[57] to take into consideration a wider and a more comprehensive purview of guidelines followed in other jurisdictions. The judicial dictum in *Anuradha Saha*[58], however, mandates the prospective application of package inserts, without the necessary constituent of such holistic incorporation.

The Summary of Product Characteristics (SPC) guidelines, laregly accepted in the European Union, provides detailed instructions to the prescriber, including the positioning of the product with regard to specific stages of the disease and therapies. The SPC also follows a more conservative approach towards dictations and warnings which further reflects its attitude towards the risk management of new pharmaceuticals. The Food and Drug Administration (FDA) does not regulate the use of a medication by a prescribing physician as the Federal Food, Drug, and

---

[55] Central Drug Authority to be on the lines of the US FDA: Ramadoss, Livemint & The Wall Street Journal, January 8, 2008

[56] Seventy-ninth Report on The Drugs and Cosmetics (Amendment) Bill 2013, Ministry of Health and Family Welfare, as presented to the Rajya Sabha on 18th December, 2013

[57] Supra notes 53 and 45

[58] Supra notes 56 and 53

Cosmetic Act does not limit the manner in which a physician may prescribe an FDA-approved medication.

The FDA recognizes that once a medication is approved for marketing, a physician may prescribe that medication for indications that are not listed in the package insert. The FDA also recognizes that there may be certain unique situations in which the appropriate and rational use of a medication may not be reflected by the package insert and may, instead, be reflected by experience and reports in the medical literature.

Medicinal variations do exist whose effect may be far more acute than as originally predicted and this may become reason for a potential finding of liability on part of physicians in unsuspecting situations such as, say, when the physician has tended only a single injection to a patient where, as per the prescribed notifications on the package insert, he may have been required to tend only two. *Dr. Laxman Balkrishna Joshi v Timbak Bapu Godbole and Anr.*[59] is a clear illustration to this, where the assistant doctor to the appellant had made the negligent assumption to inject only a single dose of morphine to a young male patient undergoing reduction treatment for a fracture, instead of injecting two as per the instruction given to him by the

---

[59] AIR 1969 SC 128

appellant; the aftermath of this was a fatal complication leading to the ultimate death of the patient.

In the backdrop of a changing medico-legal continuum in the archetypal *'West'*, the Indian medical diaspora must take care to remember that medicines are principally to be administered while keeping in consideration the respective *biophysiologic* needs and requirements of the patient undergoing the treatment, rather than a set of pre-designated guidelines or instructions pasted across the back of a random medicine container. As a further elaboration of this point, attention may be sought to a recent study carried out by the University of Oxford[60], where patients who were on opioid medication at the time had been put under an extensive examination.

Following the medication, two classes of patients could be seen to have been formed. The patients who had been on the opioid medication for two weeks were said to have developed a certain resistance or tolerance against the side effects resulting from the medication. This was defined as a phenomenon in which exposure to a drug over a long period of time results in a diminution of the actual effect of the drug or the need for a higher amount of dosage to maintain such effect. The standard postoperative opioid

---

[60] Nicola L Lewis and John E Williams, Acute Pain Management in Patients receiving Opioids for Chronic and Cancer Pain, Continuing Education in Anesthesia, Critical Care and Pain, Volume 5, Issue 4, Pages 127-129 (February, 2014)

doses were required to be based on the patient specific requirements of those who had become tolerant to the effects of the opioid as they needed larger doses of opioid in order to maintain a satisfactory level of pain relief. Physical dependence on the preoperative opioids necessitated a baseline opioid administration in the postoperative period, to prevent the occurrence of possible withdrawal reactions such as *adrenergic hyperactivity*, malaise, abdominal cramps, excessive perspiration, etc.

Thus, in the end, the postoperative baseline opioid requirement had to be calculated from the preoperative opioid consumption itself as only that could provide a suitable approximation of the opioid requirements of the patient, although actual requirements may have been a little more or less. Herefrom we observe and conclude that sometimes the measurements of a given sample of dosage must be singly determined on the basis of only a qualitative process of analysis rather than a quantitative process. However, the *Anuradha Saha*[61] judgment, as it still stands today in this regard, has restricted the medicinal treatment for an illness, sickness or disease to only the latter class of diagnosis.

---

[61] Supra notes 48 and 45

Overview

The following is a tabular representation of the changes requiring addition as already discussed above.

Aberrent element [The deteriorating influences on the health care system as discussed shall be overviewed in this section]	Recommended correction [The required corresponding changes to such influences shall be briefly looked at in this section]
1. Documenting single testimony of expert physician	a. Reports, such as that of CT scans, post mortem examinations, etc. as well as contemporary text on health issues such as journal articles and the like, be considered as expert opinion for the purposes of clinical reference b. Evidence procurement from practicing physicians be made non-mandatory, taking into account the financial implications and the time constraints relating to the same c. Common persons be selected from a multifarious range of social experiences to be made a part of the decision making process, being the first hand witnesses of the actual scenario.

2. Physicians having the free mandate to exercise preferential treatment i.e. choosing any method of treatment from a given range of others as per their own discretion	Choice of treatment methods be made in accordance with a more streamlined mechanism for such deliberation and, for this purpose, evidence based guidelines be introduced within the medical sector with the associated responsibility of every such choice made
3. Risk of exposure to illicit drug trials involving examination of drug component in the blood	a. Current Phase 1 standard of drug testing in blood be replaced with the lesser instrusive Phase 0 standard of drug test, also known as Microdosing, that does not involve the requirement of human subjects b. R & D operations in hospitals and nursing institutions be included within the ambit of 'clinical establishments' under Section 2 (c) of the Clinical Establishment Registration and Regulation Act, 2010
4. Instructions provided in the package insert of the medicine container has to be strictly complied with in strict sensu	Dosage requirements of patients be determined in accordance with their level of adaptability to intake the same

Chapter VI. Conclusion

For a disease with an unknown cause and being known to be have multiple treatment lines, there could not be a greater dearth of plausible assumptions than to depend on the opinion of only a handful of a few experts. Courts must truly allow for the proportionate amalgamation of the two disciplines of medicine and law when it comes to arbitrating on malpractice issues. As the principal forum of *'equity, good conscience and natural justice'*, it is in fact the Court's duty to invade or infiltrate the usual peripheries of ethical care treatment as is set by health professionals, and to really determine certain central standards on its own, given the colossal lack of ability on part of health professionals to empathize with the sufferings of the common.

Furthermore, the present evidential procedure in India, being fret with bias and disparity, is not one that can be matched with the standards of justice that the country's Constitution explicitly stipulates. Thus, an epidemiological approach towards evidence assimilation is prerequisite for resolving disputes arising in medical malpractice. There is also the compelling urgency to resolve the allied crisis of health care deterioration in India by adapting any such policies, principles, laws and regulations as may be suited against the present socio-economic and politico-legal realities prevailing within the country's landscape.

Although existing policies may be interpreted and moulded in whatever manner as to suit its accommodative or restrictive purpose towards incorporating changes, but the economic position of public health in the country, especially with respect to the dismal resource allocation for the same over the last five years, makes it least likely the occurrence that any actual policy change shall be effected or that the matter of revamping old, redundant policies would be taken in into the hands of the Legislators any time soon.

In that respect, having already explored how the health care reform in India can grow vis-à-vis the development of not only the national policies pertaining to the same but also the relevant judicial principles that are being developed by the courts from time to time, what remains of a curious significance still is if the courts will take notice of this inevitable nexus, the nexus being between decisions of clinical significance and the exegetical outpourings of judicial interpretations, and use it to further harness the existing clinical mechanisms in the country rather than to allow the creation of principles that act either in direct contravention of such mechanisms or principles that, while appearing to do justice in text, are simply inadequate or plain when taken in an entirely functional context.

Glossary

Immunosuppressive	Acting towards suppressing the body's natural response to the introduction of an antigen
Vasculitis	Immune complex disorder where there is inflammation of blood vessel and the consequence of such inflammation is damage and destruction to the vessel wall seen histologically as fibrinoid necrosis; it is generally treated with dapsone, prednisolone or other such immunosuppressive drugs
Toxic Epidermal Necrolysis	Blistering disorder with extensive detachment of the skin that isin most cases drug-induced, although there may be exceptions; the syndrome may involve the mucosal surfaces of the oropharynx, eyes, gastrointestinal tract, and tracheobronchial tree, resulting in dysfunction of multiple organ systems
Protean	The ability to take the assumption of several shapes and forms
Corticosteroid	Potent anti-inflmmatory drug having immunosuppressive properties
Cyclophosphamide	Anti-cancer agent that suppresses the immune system and has anti-inflammatory properties; it is not only used for treating cancer but is also used in the treatment of lupus

	when major organs such as the kidney are affected
Idiopathic	Illness or disease without a known cause or origin
Prednisolone	Corticosteroid drug that has strong anti-inflammatory properties and is used in treating inflammatory diseases such as arthritis, asthma, bronchitis and liver fibrosis among others; it can impair the immune system's ability to fight infections
Hodgkin's Lymphoma	Lymphoma that starts in the immune cells of lymph nodes and appears initially as an enlarged lymph node, gradually spreading to the organs; most lymphomas fall into the category of non-Hodgkin's disease however
Intravenous	Entering by way of, or present in, a vein; intravenous administration of medicine sends the medicine directly into the bloodstream
Avascular Necrosis	Death of a bone tissue when the blood supply to the bone is negatively affected; the bone becomes fragile and collapses under the stress of weight bearing
Crohn	Chronic inflammatory disease of the gastrointestinal tract; it is characterized by a granulomatous inflammation affecting some part of the gastrointestinal tract, with the additional tendency of forming fistulas

Multiple Sclerosis	Chronic disease of the central nervous system where there is destruction of the myelin within several regions of the brain and the spinal cord, resulting in temporary, repetitive or sustained disruptions in nerve impulse conduction
Depomedrol	Long standing drug normally used for extreme cases of asthma or arthritis, given at a maximum dosage of 40-120 mg in a 1-2 weeks interval
Pharmacological	Study of the effect of chemical substances or drugs upon living tissues
Pharmacokinetic	Documentation of the passage of drugs in the body, from the point of entry to the point of exit
Pharmacodynamic	Study of the biochemical and physiologic action of a drug on the body; the study is inclusive of the mechanism of the action of the drug
Biophysiologic	Pertaining to variables such as body temperature, blood pressure, biochemical values, blood gases and types of infection
Adrenergic Hyperactivity	Thyroid disorder falling into the class of hyperthyroidism; it is known to be a major cause of psychiatric symptoms

References

Erik S. Knusten, Ambiguous Cause-in-Fact and Structured Causation: A Multi-Jurisdictional Approach, Texas International Law Journal, Voume 38, Issue 249 (2003)

David M. Studdert, Michelle M. Mello and Troyen A. Brennan, Medical Malpractice, Health policy Report, The New England Journal of Medicine, Volume 350, Issue 3 (January 15, 2004)

Joel B. Korin and Madelyn S. Quattrone, Litigation in the Decade of Electronic Health Records, New Jersey Law Journal, 2007

Public Health, Evidence-based Policy-making and the Role of Epidemiology, Editorial, The National Medical Journal of India, Volume 26, No. 4 (2013)

U.S. Congress, Office of Technology Assessment, Defensive Medicine and Medical Malpractice, OTA-H-602 (Washington, DC: U.S. Government Printing Office, July 1994)

Harvey Teff, The Standard of Care in Medical Negligence – Moving on from Bolam?, Oxford Journal of Legal Studies, Volume 18, No. 3, Pages 473-484 (Autumn, 1998)

Joy A. Cavagnaro, Preclinical Safety Evaluation of Biopharmaceuticals: A Science Based Approach to Facilitating Clinical Trials, John Wiley & Sons (2008)

W. Jonathan Cardi, Reconstructing Forseeability, Boston College Law Review, Volume 46, No. 5, Pages 921-988 (September, 2005)

Kailash C. Mohanty, *Influence of Guidelines in Determining Medical Negligence*, British Medical Journal, Volume 330, No. 7499, Pages 1086-1087 (May 7, 2005)

Andrew Grubb, *Causation and Medical Negligence*, The Cambridge Law Journal, Volume 47, No. 3, Pages 350-352 (November, 1988)

Karunakaran Mathiharan, *Supreme Court on Medical Negligence*, Economic and Political Weekly, Volume 41, No. 2, Pages 111-115 (January, 2006)

Karyn K. Ablin, *Res Ipsa Loquitor and Expert Opinion Evidence in Medical Malpractice Cases: Strange Bedfellows*, Virginia Law Review, Volume 82, No. 2, Pages 325-355 (March, 1996)

A.C. Anand, *Speaking for Ourselves*, The National Medical Journal of India, Volume 24, No. 5 (2011)

Encyclopedia of Health, The Rosen Publishing Group, Volume 10 (2010)

Venkataram Mysore, *Dermatalogical Diseases: A Practical Approach*, BI Publications Pvt. Ltd. (January, 2007)

Richard Watts, David G. I. Scott and Chetan Mukhtyar, *Vasculitis in Clinical Practice*, Springer (May, 2015)

James E. Fitzpatrick and Joseph G. Morelli, *Dermatology Secrets Plus*, Elsevier Health Sciences (August, 2015)

Jean Louis Vincent, *Intensive Care Medicine: Annual Update 2008*, Springer Science & Business Media (Feburary, 2009)

Horace Gerald Danner, A Thesaurus of Medical Word Roots, Scarecrow Press (August, 2013)

Lupus: A Patient Care Guide for Nurses and Other Health Professionals, The Institute (2006)

Kevin R. Loughlin and Joyce A. Generali, The Guide to Off-label Prescription Drugs, Simon and Schuster (2006)

Michael Manning, Microbes Lethal to Mankind, Lulu Press (January, 2015)

Richard A. Helms and David J. Quan, Textbook of Therapeutics: Drug and Disease Management, Lippincott Williams & Wilkins (2006)

Kotwal, Textbook of Orthopaedics, Elsevier India (January, 2005)

Oxford Textbook of Medicine, Volume 1, Oxford University Press (2003)

Donald Venes, Taber's Cyclopedic Medical Dictionary, F.A. Davis Co. (2013)

Libertatem Magazine, The Law Brigade Group, Issue 1 (February, 2015)

J.G. Walton, John W. Thompson and Robin A. Seymour, Textbook of Dental Pharmacology and Therapeutics, Oxford University Press (1994)

William T. Blows, The Biological Basis of Mental Health Nursing, Routledge (December, 2010)

Kamal Kumar Sengupta and Ranabir Mukherji, *Essentials of Ocular Pharmacology and Therapy*, BI Publications (January, 2006)

Thyroid Diseases: New Insights for the Healthcare Professional, Scholarly Editions, 2011 Edition (January, 2012)

Beverley Joan Taylor, *Research in Nursing and Health Care*, Cengage Learning Australia (2006)

Jaising P. Modi, *A Text Book of Medical Jurisprudence and Toxicology*, Lexis NexisButterworths, 24th edn. (2011)

Dr. Parikh and Dr. Mishra, *The Principles of Medical Jurisprudence, Medical and Forensic Science and Technology*, CBS Publisher & Distributor (2012)

Shaun D. Pattinson, *Medical Law and Ethics*, Sweet and Maxwell, 1st edn. (2006)

YOUR KNOWLEDGE HAS VALUE